r e v i s e d

discover your conflict management style

Speed B. Leas

An Alban Institute Publication

Library of Congress Catalog Card Number 97-73981
ISBN 1-56699-184-6

09 10 11 12 13   TA   13 12 11 10 9

FOREWORD

Conflict is a part of everyone's life; we can't eliminate it. Nor would we necessarily want to–for new insights and growth can emerge from well-managed conflict. Managing conflict is something we all can do on our own, especially if we make use of techniques developed for that purpose. Healthy conflict management is a necessary part of ministry, family life, work–even play. The popularity of this book since it first appeared in 1984 is confirmation of the need for every individual to learn how best to deal with conflict.

The two-part goal of *Discover Your Conflict Management Style* remains the same as in the original version:

1. To help persons learn about the range of appropriate conflict-management strategies and when each works best.

2. To help individuals identify their own preferred styles of conflict management, and to consider using other styles as well.

What has changed in this revision is the formulation of some of the questions this resource includes to approach the two-part goal. As author Speed Leas has continued to lead workshops and conduct research on conflict management, he has had the opportunity to observe how a great variety of people use the book. The result is an even clearer and more pointed instrument than in the original.

This is a "self-help" book in the best sense of the term. It is a tool providing an entire procedure for the reader to learn about managing conflict in his or her own life. You can administer the instrument to yourself and learn your own results: the style of management that is most natural to you, and why others may seem less appealing. The manual helps you interpret your results and learn when it is most useful to employ various styles of conflict management, as well as what their likely outcomes might be. It is reassuring the learn about yourself in this regard, and to realize that there are more ways of approaching conflict than you might have experienced. You can use this information to improve relations in all facets of your life.

As Speed Leas points out, the appropriate time to use this resource is not in the midst of a conflict–but at a time when you can contemplate and digest the information for future use. You might set aside a period of time during which you administer the instrument, and then ponder the additional resources for interpreting it and putting the results to good use. In this revision, you will benefit from the author's most recent insights in conflict management for religious groups. Even if you have used the earlier version, you will want to work with this one as well. There is probably no more or less conflict today than there has ever been in human relations–but through the accumulated wisdom of experts like Leas, we become ever more capable of using it in healthy, growth-producing ways.

Linda-Marie Delloff
Director of Publishing

ACKNOWLEDGMENTS

For a number of years, I used a variety of instruments for assessing an individual's usual or preferred conflict styles. None of these was fully satisfactory. So, drawing on the learning and the concepts from those who have gone before me, I developed another tool for helping people look at their conflict behavior.

I am indebted to the writers of two conflict instruments that I have used extensively and from which I have drawn many of the ideas that are contained herein:

Conflict Management Survey, by Jay Hall, published by Teleometrics Int'l., P.O. Box 314, The Woodlands, TX 77380.

Thomas-Kilmann Conflict Mode Instrument, by Kenneth W. Thomas and Ralph H. Kilmann, published by XICOM, Sterling Forest, Tuxedo, NY 10987.

Before You Begin

You want to gain insights into your conflict management style? I suggest you fill out the Conflict Inventory at the back of this book.

This instrument has been developed to meet two objectives, to help people:

- become aware of the range of appropriate conflict strategies available to them and when each is appropriate to use;
- become aware of their own preferred styles and reflect on other possible styles they might choose to use more frequently.

This questionnaire is not meant to be a "personality inventory" that can be relied on to probe the inner workings of a person's mind or emotions. A person's conflict style changes dramatically from situation to situation. Someone's behavior will change depending on whom they are arguing with, what the stakes are, and the norms of the situation. (Yelling is okay at a baseball game, but not in a board meeting.) So it is not recommended that one assume that one's "style" is likely to be the same at home, at work, and in a community organization.

Nor do I make any claims about this inventory being "scientifically valid." It is meant only to help the user develop some language to talk about conflict and to reflect on how it can be managed.

This inventory can profitably be used in a number of settings. It can be taken alone, without reference to or conversation with other people. After filling out the form, a person can fill out the score sheet on page 43 and then read the interpretation of the scores without talking with anyone else. It can also be used in conjunction with couples or groups. Asking each person in the relationship or group to fill out the instrument in his or her copy of this publication and then sharing personal "scores" with each other can be enlightening in terms of improved understanding of the relationship. Some people in very small groups have filled out the instrument reflecting on their own behavior, and then filled out a separate form reflecting on the behavior of their teammates. This can be particularly helpful in giving and receiving feedback on your conflict behaviors.

Discover Your Conflict Management Style was developed primarily for use in churches and synagogues to help members gain insight and skill in dealing with conflicts before they become overly difficult or nasty. You can use this instrument to help members of a congregation or a board become more comfortable with differences and to encourage open and confident sharing of differences and concerns with one another.

A word of caution before you begin: It is not recommended that you attempt to use this instrument in groups or within relationships that are seriously troubled. For the learning to be meaningful, those using this inventory should have some trust between or among them and not be likely to use the gathered insights about someone as a means of further attack and belittling.

Go ahead. Read the following instrument instructions. Answer the questions (see page 35) and figure your score. Do not read the scoring sheets or proceed to the following interpretive text until you have completed the Conflict Inventory.

Instructions

As you answer the questions on the inventory, think of yourself in a particular conflict "setting," by this I mean a setting in which you are sometimes or often in conflict. Do not attempt to think of yourself "in general" or in a variety of settings, but in one particular environment. A *setting* is an environment, organization, or relationship that has significance for you as distinct from other settings or relationships. For example, a setting might be your relationship with your spouse as distinct from your relationship with your children; it might be your relationships with your co-workers or with your boss; it might be your relationships in your church or synagogue, or on a particular community board.

I have found people get different scores as they think of themselves in each setting. So, if you want to reflect on your conflict behavior at work, and you have filled out this instrument using your understanding of yourself at home, you'll need to answer the questions a second time to explore your behavior in the work environment.

It is not a good idea to choose answers based on one particular conflict that may have occurred in your chosen setting. Rather, think in terms of several conflicts that may have occurred in that setting. Also, do not choose the worst conflicts you have experienced in this setting. Try to reflect on yourself in the usual and regular situations that you get into, not those that have been particularly tough or easy. On another occasion, you can fill the inventory out on a particularly difficult or easy conflict.

For each question give an answer that reflects, as close as it can, how you usually respond in this conflict setting. Each question contains a pair of statements describing possible behavior responses. For each pair, *circle the "A" or "B" statement that is most characteristic* of your own behavior. In many cases neither "A" nor "B" may be very typical of your behavior; even so, please select the response you would be more likely to make. If you skip questions, the scoring will not be meaningful.

After you have completed and scored the instrument, return to the body of this booklet for explanatory insights that will help you become more effective in various conflict situations.

Interpreting Your Score

Note: Do not read until you have completed the Conflict Inventory (see page 35).

This instrument identifies six different styles for managing differences: *Persuading, Compelling, Avoiding/Accommodating, Collaborating, Negotiating,* and *Supporting.* Each can be an appropriate style, and none should be thought of as "bad" or inferior. A certain style can cause a problem when it is used inappropriately, but one should not assume that Avoiding is always wrong or that all conflicts must be confronted. Nor should one assume that Compelling is always inappropriate or that one should make an effort in every situation to collaborate or persuade. In fact, the styles that have been recently touted as always appropriate can be harmful when they are used in contexts that call for other strategies. (For example, using collaborative strategies is inappropriate in situations where people will take advantage of naive people who may become inappropriately vulnerable. Collaboration is also inappropriate when both sides will not or cannot share all information.)

On each scale in this instrument, it is possible for you to score from 0 to 15. The lower your score, the less likely you are to choose this particular strategy or style; the higher your score, the more likely you are to use this style.

The style on which you received the highest score indicates the style with which you feel most comfortable in your "chosen" setting. The lowest score names the style with which you are least comfortable in this setting. The theory of the inventory is that you are likely to behave more in the modes of your high scores and less in the modes of your low scores.

Your "conflict profile" is all of your style scores compared with one another. To interpret your profile, notice the range of differences among your scores. If your second-ranked score is only one number lower than your highest-ranked score, it will probably be fairly easy for you to choose the second-highest strategy as a backup when your first choice seems not to be working. But if the difference is three or more, you will tend to hold on longer to the strategy with the higher score, even when it is not working because it is significantly preferred over the strategy with the lower score. Strategies for which you have very low scores will be difficult for you to use in the chosen setting.

Let's look at some examples. Here is one woman's profile:

Persuading - 10
Compelling - 4
Avoiding/Accommodating - 5
Collaborating - 12
Negotiating -7
Supporting - 7

This profile shows a preference for Collaboration and Persuasion in dealing with conflict. The closeness of the two high scores (12 and 10) means that it will be fairly easy for her to choose either style and perhaps use the two in conjunction with each other. The difference between the Persuasion score (10) and the score for Negotiating (7) and Supporting (7), however, is three; this means that it will be difficult for this person to shift into the Negotiating or Supporting mode if Collaboration and Persuading don't work. (It will be very difficult indeed for her to use Compelling behaviors in the setting she was thinking about.)

Here is another example:

Persuading - 3
Compelling - 2
Avoiding/Accommodating - 2
Collaborating - 10
Negotiating - 14
Supporting - 14

Here we have a man who has two scores tied for the highest mark. This means he may feel conflicted—as to whether to negotiate or support—before he will be able to enter into the conflict management process. Though he has a relatively high score of 10 for Collaboration, there is a substantial difference (of four) between the two highest scores (14) and the second highest (10). This person probably would delay significantly before using this Collaboration strategy, even though it is preferred above others. Of course, the extremely low scores for Persuading, Compelling, and Avoiding/Accommodating mean that these styles would be virtually impossible for him to use.

Here is one more example:

Persuading - 7
Compelling - 6
Avoiding/Accommodating - 7
Collaborating - 9
Negotiating - 8
Supporting - 8

These scores, as you can see, are very close together, with a total difference between the highest score (9) and the lowest (6) of three. It will not be difficult for this person to use any of the styles in the instrument. This person has the most flexibility of the three discussed in these examples. If a wide variety of resources in a constantly changing environment is needed, this score would be ideal. But in situations that call for a decided skill in one area, this person may not have enough "stuff" in that arena to perform well.

Choosing a Conflict Management Strategy

Persuading

As a style of managing differences, Persuasion has not been addressed much in recent years; it has been held in disrepute by a number of conflict theorists, especially those—such as Rensis Likert,[1] William Dyer,[2] and Alan Filley[3]—who tout collaborative approaches to dealing with differences. Yet I sense that persuasive strategies are the most frequently used of all the conflict management strategies. (Indeed, they are the most frequently misused strategies.)

Persuasion strategies are those where a person or group attempts to change another's point of view, way of thinking, feelings, or ideas. One attempting to persuade another uses rational approaches, deductive and inductive argument, and any other verbal means she thinks will work to convince the other that her opinion is the one that should prevail.

When one chooses to use a persuasive strategy in conflict, one assumes that the other is incorrect or ignorant and needs to be changed in order to improve the situation, the relationship, the organization, or the individual. The persuader does not assume that she needs to change, that she needs to act or think differently. The only one who is expected to change is the target of the persuasive behavior.

Persuasion is quite different from Negotiation or Collaboration, where it is assumed that all of the parties to the conflict are going to have to share in the change.

How to Persuade

Many books and articles have been written on the subject of persuasive argument, especially for debaters and salespeople. Some of the following advice comes from my own observation, and some is noted from laboratory or field experiments. Within the limited scope of this inventory, we can only skim some of the more important learning. If you want to persuade, these pointers can help you do it appropriately and well.

Try specifically to meet the needs of the other—the target of your persuasive activities. Many conflict practitioners and theorists have expanded on this point, including Gerard Nierenberg,[4] Chester Karrass,[5] and Roger Fisher and William Ury.[6] They say that if you want to influence another person, you must know what that person wants, what his interests are. As Fisher and Ury say in their book, "The basic problem in a negotiation lies not in conflict positions, but in the conflict between each side's needs, desires, concerns, and fears."[7] They describe a "position" as the individual's or group's conclusion as to how needs can be met. Fisher and Ury define "needs" as interests. They believe that Persuasion is most effective when you understand the problem the other is facing (the need or interest), and you respond to that rather than to the position or solution the other is proposing. Responding to the position alone does not help the other perceive that you appreciate what she is up against, and it may keep you stuck until you can find a solution (position) that meets both the needs of the other and yourself.

Present both sides. When sensing conflict, we tend to downplay or denigrate the position of the other and enhance our own position. This only makes Persuasion more difficult. The other resists our arguments because he does not think we understand or appreciate his position. But when we move against our own tendency to be self-protective and one-sided, we are inviting the other to respond in kind. Appreciation goes a long way toward helping Persuasion be effective. Recognizing the good points of the other's position is appreciation that is appreciated.

Present your favored viewpoint last. People tend to remember and respond to what they heard last. If you put your best argument at the beginning of the discussion, the other will not remember it and will be responding to things that you said later rather than that which you really wanted her to take seriously. Save your best "shot" for the time when it will be best remembered and dealt with.

Be for, not against. Here again, we know that a positive approach is more effective than a negative approach—against which one has to be protected. Those who are best able to persuade are those who are attractive; negative people and negative arguments tend not to attract others.

Do not interrupt. Seems like simple and hackneyed advice, but it is difficult to practice. Letting the other have his say is another way of appreciating the other and what the other has to say.

Do not hurry to make your points. Rushing, pushing, or crowding is not persuasive; it is experienced as Compelling, which generates resistance to you and your arguments. Taking time, approaching an argument with ease and comfort, will generate trust on the part of the other in you and your argument.

Cover one point at a time. If you are trying to persuade somebody of something, that person is more likely to be persuaded one small point at a time, rather than by your trying to skip hurriedly over the little points that make up the argument for the whole. Build a foundation and step by step move toward your goal.

Know your key points and keep coming back to them. When I noted the importance of making your best point last, I recommended this as a mnemonic device. Repetition is also effective as an assist to the memory. Even more important than repetition and saving your best argument for last, however, is to know your facts. Start by knowing what you are talking about. This may not only impress those you are trying to persuade, but it may also lower your own sense of inadequacy to the point where your anxiety will not be telegraphed to the other, corrupting your ability to persuade.

When to Persuade

While persuasive strategies are attractive to many of us and we are quick to use them, they are often inappropriate, especially in higher levels of conflict. Behavioral science research has been finding that Persuasion tends not to work in situations of low trust. In other words, as the conflict increases, the trust decreases, and the less likely people are to listen to, let alone be persuaded by, what their opponent or enemy has to say.

If you are going to try to change someone else's way of thinking, you are most likely to be successful under these conditions:

- the other is unclear about what he wants;
- the other trusts your motives;
- you have prestige and competence in the other's eyes;
- the other perceives your goals and hers to be compatible;
- the other perceives herself to be appreciated or respected by you;
- the other does not have strong needs for independence and self-competence;
- the other does not have strong opinions on the subject.

There are two other conditions that will affect your choice of a Persuading strategy: your own willingness to change or compromise in the situation, and whether Collaborating or Negotiating strategies are available to you.

Let's look at these two conditions, one at a time. Your willingness to change centers on your perception of the problem. How do you see the problem? Is there any need or reason for you to change your behavior or the way you are thinking about this subject? If you believe that it is unnecessary for you to change and that it is only the other who must do the changing, Collaboration or Negotiation is likely not possible. If you can see "the handwriting on the wall" and don't want to change but know that you must, it is possible to collaborate or negotiate. It is not possible to collaborate or negotiate without some willingness on your part to bend or change. If you are not going to bend, then Persuasion, Compelling, and Avoiding are about the only choices you have.

Let me put this another way. Persuasion is used when you don't see the problem as "your" problem; you think it "belongs" to someone else, and therefore you don't expect to modify your behavior or your thinking. When the difficulty that we are experiencing is "ours," then *we* have the possibility of doing something about it. So the husband who says he is unhappy with the marriage but is unwilling to do anything to change his own behavior cannot collaborate or negotiate; he can attempt only to compel or persuade.

When considering persuasive strategies, determine whether collaborative or negotiative strategies are open to you. In some situations it is not possible to negotiate or collaborate, even when you are willing to change your own behavior or thinking, such as (1) when it is not possible for you to be fully open with another person (this would preclude

Collaboration but not Negotiation), (2) when you or the other parties involved don't have sufficient skill, tolerance, or experience at Collaboration to be able to use this mode, (3) when repeated and significant attempts have been made to collaborate or negotiate and these have failed. In these circumstances you may have to turn to Persuasion or Compelling as your only alternative strategies.

Probable Outcomes of Persuasion Strategies

Persuasion strategies can be very disappointing. Often, when we hope to convince others of doing things that are "for their own good" and/or for the good of the organization, they give verbal assent while they are with us, but they don't follow through when they are not in our presence. Much has been written about power in organizations and relationships, and people are continuously clamoring to find ways to make people do things without actually compelling them. This is the problem with Persuasion. One hopes the other will comply, but argument without authority often seems weak and inadequate in the face of those who have the power and right to override our recommendations when they choose.

Further, it is precisely when trust is low and resistance is high that we wish we could influence another person through Persuasion. But these are the situations in which Persuasion is least likely to be effective. What is the alternative? It is improving the relationship and the trust level before you attempt to change the behavior or thinking of the other. Without the other party's strong commitment to you and belief in the efficacy of your words, your attempts to persuade are likely to result in very little change.

Though we should not discount Persuasion as an effective conflict management tool, it is more likely to be effective with people already "on your side" than it is with "the opposition" (especially in high conflict), and it will not be useful until significant work has been done in relationship building.

Compelling or Forcing

I define *Compelling* as the use of physical or emotional force, authority, or pressure to oblige or constrain one party to do something another party wants done. (Note that I did not say or imply that you can compel a person to *think* a certain way. I don't believe that is possible. People can, however, be compelled to *act* according to the wishes of those with the most authority, power, or physical force.)

Most of the Compelling we experience in our day-to-day lives is not through the use of physical force but that which comes through the use of authority. Authority is the right we give to a person or group to make certain decisions for us—because it is expedient or because we can't agree. Authority comes through a tacit or explicit contract we make with others. For example, when people join an organization, they discover it has an explicit contract (constitution or bylaws) by which the members are expected to abide. This contract sets forth the rules of the game by which people will play and authorizes certain groups or people to make certain decisions for the rest of the group; for example, the president names the nominating committee; the treasurer prepares the trial budget for the following year; and so on. There are also many tacit contracts in an organization or relationship: "We've always done it that way" is one; social mutual understandings of roles, such as those of mothers and fathers, is another. Authority is the understanding we have of who is responsible for what, and we let people exercise certain influence within the bounds of that understanding. Of course, when a person steps beyond the bounds of that mutually understood authority, tacit or explicit, that person's authority is compromised and the ability to compel or force is significantly diminished.

What are some examples of Compelling using explicit authority?

- a police officer pulling a motorist to the curb and giving the driver a ticket;
- a pastor explaining to a couple that she will not marry them because she does not think they are yet mature enough to understand or carry out a long-term mutual commitment;
- a doctor admitting a patient to the hospital;
- an arbiter telling each side what it will get out of a particular settlement.

What are some examples of the use of tacit authority?

- a parent telling a child to pick up his room;
- a consultant telling the members of a group to be quiet so they can hear one another.

One question comes before almost every person in a conflict situation: Is it okay to use *Compelling* strategies? As with most questions in life, the answer is "It all depends." We have learned a great deal about the impact on others of Compelling behaviors, and we know that if they are used consistently over a long period of time, people suffer, relationships deteriorate, people lose their spontaneity, manipulative behavior develops, and rebellions simmer or break out. But there are times when Compelling behavior is needed and/or wanted within an organization or within a relationship. These will be discussed below. The point I make here is that Compelling is like the use of certain drugs: In short-term emergencies they are sometimes called for, when nothing else will probably work. But in the long term, Compelling is caustic and rots out relationships and organizations.

How to Compel or Force

To increase your success at Compelling behavior, increase your authority, both tacit and explicit. As we all know, it can be to the advantage of an influencer of policy to have the rules changed so that she or he is given the right to make more decisions in the organization. But your authority can also be enhanced by increasing your knowledge about a particular subject, by increasing your assertiveness, and by increasing the size of the audience favorable to your point of view. Audiences are a significant force in organizational dynamics. To the extent that one perceives himself to be under the scrutiny of either many people or certain people particularly respected by the rest of the organization, that person will likely act in ways designed to please these people—this audience. So one way to increase your power in the organization is to get those who are already viewed as authorities to agree with you. This is one way to increase the size of the audiences that might agree with your position.

Of course, the clearer you are about what it is that you want— your goals, your standards, your values, your expectations—the greater your ability to compel others will be. Nothing will vitiate your ability to influence others more than your own unclarity about what it is that should be done.

The chances of your Compelling behavior having an impact increase to the extent that you can keep control of the conversation and keep the initiative in the argument. If and as you lose the initiative, you are put more on the defensive; more of your energies go to protecting yourself rather than getting the change that you want in others.

Compelling behavior also seems to "stick" better when you end the conversation when it is finished, rather than going back over ground that has already been covered or attempting to move into "softer" modes such as Persuasion. As the compeller tries to tone down or sweeten the style, he or she is likely to diminish his or her power.

Of course, the compeller will need to be clear about what the consequences are, if what is being "requested" is not complied with. The essence of Compelling lies in the fact that the compeller is able to bring sanctions to bear against the individual or group being compelled. If you cannot bring sanctions, you are not literally compelling the other. Some people threaten consequences they could theoretically bring to pass, but it is known that the threats are empty. This is not Compelling behavior. It will have little, if any, impact on others if they don't believe you can or will implement your threats.

If you want your threats to have meaning in the future, you will want to be sure that you bring sanctions to bear immediately upon noncompliance with your demands. This will show that when you say something, you are not just mouthing words; you will follow through on your statements; your words are more likely to be believed and to have more tacit authority.

Compelling behavior is further enhanced by the avoidance of qualifying words such as *I hope; I wish; perhaps; wouldn't it be a good idea if...; in my opinion.* These phrases take the punch out of the more direct, authoritative statement that lets the other know where you are coming from and demands a clear response. The rule here is: A clear statement will get a clear response (not always what you want, but at least you will know where you stand). You may think you are clear, but that doesn't always mean that you are clear, so it is always a good idea to check to see whether or not you have been understood. Check to see that the other understands you by requesting some kind of statement that will indicate to you that he knows how to comply.

When to Use Compelling

Infrequently. Because of the problems that come with regular use of this strategy, you will find that it is more effective and that people will respond better when these strategies are used sparingly.

When you or others are being threatened or are under attack. This is the time to call such strategies into play—under emergency conditions. Assuming that these conditions won't last long, you respond with appropriate authority and force to protect what is being threatened.

When rights are being violated. Here again, we are talking about threat and attack. In situations of injustice, when other means have failed, it is appropriate to increase the level of pressure to a point where justice is in place.

When you have tacit or explicit authority to demand compliance. If you don't have the legal or understood right to demand compliance to your "requests," you are likely to be ignored, condemned, or punished for infringement on the authority of others. In other words, do not use Compelling behavior when it is out of bounds for you. If you can do it legally, it may well be appreciated, but when this is not the case it is best to move toward other methods of dealing with conflict.

When you can call in authority. When you don't have the authority yourself to demand compliance, there are occasions when others do have the authority needed to deal with a troublesome situation. They should be called in to help deal with the problem.

When the other believes you will use your authority. Of course, you will have little or no compelling impact on another if that person does not believe you will use your rights to bring sanctions. Past history and present conditions may strongly affect this parameter.

When there is inadequate time to work through the differences.
It is usually best to use other means of managing conflict than Compelling, because of the caustic effect it has on organizations, relationships,
and people. It should be chosen only under emergency conditions.

When and where all other means have failed. After trying and
trying to work through differences, perceiving that none of them has
worked, and seeing that ways need to be found for the people in the
system to live together or at least get along in nonaggressive ways, you
may determine to exercise authority to limit and control the aggressive
behaviors of the various parties.

When one is able to monitor performance. Only behavior that
can be observed can be compelled. If you are not able to determine
whether your demands have been complied with, you had better use an
approach other than Compelling.

***When performance is easily evaluated and can be evaluated
promptly.*** Here again, Compelling that which is vague and general has
the same difficulties as being unable to monitor performance. One can
compel a salesperson to make ten calls per day (this is easily evaluated),
but one cannot compel a pleasant manner.

On important, unpopular courses of action. Finally, in some
situations for which you hold responsibility, when others are not going
to agree with a decision because it seriously affects their self-interest,
you will have to enter a Compelling mode. Examples of this include:
cost cutting, terminating employees, disciplining staff. It is sometimes
best to use your authority in the beginning and get the painful process
over with. To start with what looks like open, collaborative approaches
to a problem that in the end will not be collaborative is manipulative.

Probable Outcomes of Compelling Strategies

The results of Compelling have been implicitly and explicitly stated
above, but I summarize them here:

- Compliance will occur only under direct supervision and
  regular inspection.

- Compelled people or groups are not likely to continue doing what has been demanded of them when they believe the sanctions have been removed.
- Morale will be low in organizations that continually use compelling.
- Compelled people or groups are likely to seek means of increasing their own power and independence through the use of sabotage or other means of getting revenge.

Avoiding, Ignoring, Accommodating, or Fleeing

Under this third category I have included four distinct conflict management styles or strategies. I could have developed this instrument in a way that would have separated these four styles. We would than have ended up with nine categories of conflict strategies. This would have required us to remember too many categories (six is almost too many, as it is) and answer too many questions—108—more than twice as many. To avoid these problems I combined four categories defined as follows under the heading Avoiding/Accommodating.

Avoiding

When one avoids conflict, one evades it or stays away from it. One attempts to skirt it or keep it from happening. Putting a tricky agenda item late in the meeting in hopes that you won't get to it, not bringing up an uncomfortable subject, attempting to keep people who might bring up "the" subject from speaking—all are examples of Avoidance.

Ignoring

Ignoring a conflict is acting as if it weren't going on. Most people aren't able to do this very well. Leaders in an organization may ignore conflict by never putting the issue on agenda and talking about "it" only before or after the meetings.

Fleeing

Ignoring (above) is the only passive strategy for dealing with conflict. Avoidance takes effort and attention to what is happening; so does fleeing.

Fleeing is actively removing yourself from the arena in which conflict might take place. As a conflict management strategy, fleeing can occur before or during a conflict. If it occurs after the conflict has taken place, it would be a result of conflict not a conflict management strategy.

Accommodating

This is another active strategy. When you accommodate, you go along with the other, with the opposition. A person using an accommodative style often sees the relationship as being more important than the issue. So as not to jeopardize the relationship, this person may shrink from any confrontation that "dealing with the issue" might require. Often, sup-pressing the feelings that arise when you are not able to get what you want because you choose to go along with what the other wants requires self-control. Another phrase for *accommodation* could be "giving in." (Avoidance, ignoring, and fleeing are also forms of "giving in," in that they allow the status quo to stand; they don't change the situation in any way.)

How to Avoid, Ignore, Accommodate, or Flee

Procrastination is a common strategy used to avoid, ignore, or accom-modate. Putting off dealing with the conflict may be the most common way that this set of strategies is used.

Another way of implementing these strategies is by saying yes to every request that is made of you and then just not doing it. Note that this is not really Accommodation, though it seems so on the surface. Accommodation means actually going through with what the other wants you to do. Saying one thing and doing another is ignoring.

Another ignoring strategy is to use Support strategies when you should be using Collaboration, Negotiation, Compelling, or Persuasion. We'll discuss Support strategies a little later. At this point suffice it to say that if you are a part of the problem or are fully or partly responsible for how it gets dealt with, your paraphrasing and showing concern for the feelings of the other but without responding to the problem, is in fact ignoring or avoiding the problem. Submitting your resignation is fleeing. Threatening to submit your resignation unless you get your way is Compelling.

Of course, a time-honored bureaucratic Avoidance strategy is to study the problem with no intention of doing anything about it.

When to Use Avoiding, Ignoring, Accommodating, or Fleeing Strategies

While the manner in which I have described the Avoidance/Accommodation strategies above tends not to be respectful of their use, there are many occasions when it is indeed useful and appropriate to employ them.

Sometimes the *cost* of working a problem through is greater than the *value* of having worked it through. In those cases, these strategies would be the right choice.

When people within the organization or relationship are particularly fragile and insecure, you may choose not to "work" certain issues because doing so would cause too much damage.

When people need time or "space" to cool down, avoidance is sometimes appropriate.

When there is conflict on many fronts, you may want to avoid certain areas of conflict to devote your energy to others.

When the differences are trivial or irrelevant to your relationship or the organization, they are often best avoided.

When the parties in a conflict are unable or unwilling to reconcile their differences or attempt to work them through and they must continue to be in the same place or to work together, Avoidance, Accommodating, and/or Ignoring are the only choices available.

When you don't care about the relationship and the quality of interaction within it, Avoidance or Fleeing is appropriate.

When you are powerless to effect change of any kind, when the other does not or will not respond, and repeated efforts have been made to invite the other to address the issues with you and try to work them through, then Fleeing (leaving) is the only choice. Notice here that the key word is *powerless*. Don't underestimate your power and the resources available to you with the result that you too quickly bail out of a relationship that could be salvaged.

Probable Outcomes

The most serious problem with this cluster of conflict strategies is that they don't change anything—and usually they don't help. When one chooses to avoid, accommodate, flee, or ignore, one lets things remain as they are: What is unjust remains unjust; what is unfair remains unfair; and what is disrespectful remains disrespectful.

We believe that people we respect can stand up to and grow from a loving confrontation. Avoiding says, "I have given up on you and the relationship at this point. I don't think it, you, or I can improve or change." Thus the element of disrespect.

Usually organizations and people that regularly use these strategies are depressed and remain depressed. The people don't feel good about themselves and use much of their energy restraining themselves.

Collaborating

Collaborative conflict strategies are frequently touted as the best or only strategy to use when dealing with conflict. As I have indicated above, it is only the best strategy in situations that appropriately call for its use. When one collaborates, one co-labors, works together, with others on the resolution of the difficulties that are being experienced. In a conflict situation, Collaboration means that you work together with the people with whom you disagree. You might call Collaboration "joint problem solving" or "mutual problem solving" because that is the essence of what a collaborative strategy is.

How to Collaborate

When using a collaborative approach to dealing with conflict, the following steps must be carried out by all parties to the conflict. Where any step is taken without the involvement of the others in the conflict setting, it must be repeated *with the others* if the solution is to be truly collaborative.

- Jointly acknowledge that there is a problem.
- Jointly agree on ground rules.
- Jointly agree on process for dealing with the problem.
- Jointly define the problem(s).
- Jointly identify shared interests.
- Jointly invent options for *mutual* gain.
- Jointly agree on criteria for choosing among the options.
- Jointly choose an option or options.

In their book *Interpersonal Conflict,* Hocker and Wilmont give an example of how a couple facing conflict might collaborate. The wife complains that her husband gives too much time and attention to his work and not enough to her. The husband complains that his wife shows precious little interest in his work. One solution might be the husband working fewer hours and spending more time at home; the wife would ask questions about his work life. But Collaboration goes further, with husband and wife together trying to identify individual issues behind the conflict. Do they both "want more warmth and affection in the relationship"? If so, how can they both "go for" meeting those needs? As they collaborate, "they explore the disagreement...to learn from one another's insights." Maybe it's important that they give each other undivided attention at a specified time. "They may be able to meet for lunch occasionally and then the husband can work at home late on an evening. Collaboration as a style means that one person asserts individual goals while being concerned with the goals of the other also." [8]

When to Use Collaboration

Choose collaborative strategies in situations where you and the others involved are willing to play by collaborative rules; that is, all the parties involved in the conflict must be willing and able to acknowledge that there is a problem, to share all the information each individual or group has about the problem, and to stick with a problem-solving process. Otherwise it will not be possible for one individual (or group) or several people (or groups) to "collaborate" while the others are doing something else. All the parties must be able to enter into this mode.

All of the parties must be willing and able to come to sessions where the issues will be discussed. And there must be a good deal of motivation on each group's part to stick with the problem-solving process once it is under way. This will take stick-to-it-iveness on the part of everybody concerned because it often seems easier to move out of the collaboration and on to quicker (and what seem in the short run to be more satisfying) modes to use, Persuasion and Compelling.

So Collaboration should be used when the stakes are high and the costs of not collaborating greatly exceed the costs of directly confronting the issues and trying to work them through with people with whom you initially disagree.

Individual predilections can interfere with a group's ability to collaborate. What's more, the norms or unwritten rules of the organization sometimes conspire against Collaboration. Often the group is well trained to believe *Robert's Rules* is the only recourse when the going gets rough, and these rules assume Persuasion and Compelling as the major means of dealing with difference. Overcoming these norms (and sometimes written policies about how to proceed in conflict) may be a formidable challenge in itself.

Collaboration takes time, so there has to be enough time available to use this method.

And sometimes the *issue* will affect whether or not it is possible to collaborate. Dichotomous issues (issues where only two choices exist, such as whether or not to fire a staff person) cannot be worked collaboratively. Such an issue must be changed to one that will allow Collaboration; for example, the question might be changed to "How can this staff person's performance be improved?"

Further, conflict over limited resources, where the resources are inadequate to meet fully every party's needs, cannot be dealt with collaboratively. These kinds of conflicts require Negotiation rather than Collaboration. Collaboration assumes that we will be able to find solutions that will be mutually satisfying to all the parties, which, as we all know, is not always possible.

Finally, Collaboration is probably not going to be possible in high-conflict settings. Where fear and distrust are at exceptionally high levels, emotion is likely to cloud people's ability to share fully with one another and genuinely engage in a joint problem-solving process.

Likely Outcomes of Collaboration

Behavioral scientists and others who study conflict are so keen on collaborative strategies because the likelihood of real success is greatly increased when people are able to join in mutual problem solving. That's to say:

- People will have high motivation to comply with their joint decisions
- The quality of decisions is usually significantly increased.
- People's problem-solving abilities are usually strengthened.
- All the parties to the original conflict usually walk away from it with a sense of satisfaction and success: "We did it!"

Collaboration goes for solutions in which all parties "win."

Bargaining or Negotiating

I use the words *bargain* and *negotiate* interchangeably; they mean virtually the same thing. Bargaining or Negotiation refer to a strategy that is very similar to Collaboration, except that the expectations of the parties are lower as they enter the conflict arena. Instead of seeking solutions that are mutually fulfilling to both or all parties, people who use Negotiation are trying to get as much as they can, assuming that they will not get everything they want (but at least they will get some of what they want, as the others get some of what they want). In other words, where Collaboration is a win-win strategy, Negotiation is a sorta-win-sorta-lose strategy.

How to Bargain

Bargaining is the art of backing off; it is a process of making demands that you do not expect to be fulfilled, with the intention of getting less than you would really like to have while satisfying some of the needs the other bargainer brings to the table. In labor-management negotiations, "good faith" bargaining is often defined by whether or not a party has shown "progress" in the negotiations through willingness to back off from some of the original demands. If a party has not reduced the original demand or demands in some way, the other side or people monitoring the process may call "foul" because of the unwillingness to reduce the original demands.

Because of this need to prepare to settle for less at the beginning of the bargaining process, some bargainers may start with outlandish demands in order to end up with a satisfactory settlement. Of course, when this is taken to an extreme, the other bargainers find this behavior offensive, and they not only have diminished trust, but sometimes have become quite hostile. This makes bargaining even more difficult.

To do a good job of bargaining, the parties involved must share some information. I previously indicated that in Collaboration, the parties must share all the information each has; there must not be secret or privileged information withheld from the other party. But in bargaining, this is not the case. We do not expect the other side to share everything, nor do we share everything; we share only that which we think will be helpful to our case. This reluctance to share reduces trust between the parties, but it is understood as one of the givens of this style of conflict management—and because it is expected, the withholding of information is not likely to be as harmful to the process as it would be in a situation where the parties assume that the other will be open and fully disclose everything relevant to the case.

Many experts propose that the negotiators start with the easy issues first when a number of problems are to be resolved. Starting with things we can agree on can help generate mutual optimism about our ability to work things through, and it can help us be less defensive.

Effective bargainers also find they are helped by a process in which the negotiators stress the similarities of their positions rather than their differences. To reach agreement the parties will have to believe that agreement is possible and well within the realm of reasonable and responsible action. To the extent that the bargainers are not optimistic about this fact, they are likely to reduce their efforts to look for solutions that incorporate some payoffs for all sides.

Bargainers are also helped by stressing the desirability of agreement. When you are in a conflict with another person and that individual doesn't seem to be entering into the conversation in a way that leads you to believe you will be able to find agreement, you may become discouraged and begin to believe the whole business is hopeless. It is from such a despairing stance that belligerent and hard-line positions are likely to escalate tensions. The more you can let the other know that you really want agreement and are committed to finding solutions that are reasonably satisfying to everyone concerned, the less likely that the negotiations will break down or turn into a mutually compelling situation from which no one is likely to benefit.

Bargainers who present positive points about the other's argument before the other does, or who acknowledge the good points that the other is bringing to the conversation, are more likely to be influential than those who argue only for their own position and against the other. If you present both sides and are truly convinced that, on balance, your position is the better one, you will be better able to argue persuasively.

Present your best points last. Most researchers who have studied Negotiation will tell you that your audience will probably not remember everything you have said. Hearers are most likely to retain what they heard last. So if you want the other to be influenced by what you say, use your best material close to end of your presentation.

Finally, don't rely on innuendo or unspecified implications of an argument to get the point across. Be very clear about your conclusions. When you let your audience decide what you mean, the audience can decide almost anything. If you want to influence the audience to end up where you are, tell them clearly where you are and how you got there.

When to Use Bargaining

While Collaboration is a strategy that you can use in lower levels of conflict, Negotiation can be used at all levels. People are used to it, they expect it, and they usually know how to deal with it. A frequent problem with the use of Negotiation, however, is the fact that many issues or problems are not negotiable. For example, when parties have absolutely mutually exclusive (or dichotomous) goals, it is impossible to bargain. Take the case of an argument over whether or not to ordain women to the ministry. This is not an issue you can bargain over because there is no possibility of backing off from your original demand. Either you are for it or against it; you can't have it part way. There are some issues where it might be technically possible to negotiate, but the values and sensibilities of the participants would be so offended that Negotiation would be perceived as anathema. When people hold commitments to certain values or theological stances, encouraging them to "compromise" is likely to be perceived as immoral. In these cases you will have to stay with either Persuasion or Collaboration.

To bargain, the "prize" must be something that is divisible or items one can trade. For example, it was not possible for the two women to bargain over the baby brought before Solomon. With only one baby, the only "backing down" they could do was 100 percent backing down. Compromise was not possible.

You will find Compromise strategies to be acceptable and useful in cases where Compelling is not appropriate and Collaboration has been tried and has failed (or you don't think it is possible to try it, because you won't be able to get everyone to share all the information). Often Compelling strategies are too costly to use, in that they take a great deal of time and energy to monitor the "agreements" and the parties are likely resistant to carrying out compelled demands. So Negotiation is often a good compromise between Collaboration and Compelling.

To be able to bargain, it is necessary for all the parties to be willing to bargain. It is not possible for one side to bargain alone. All the parties must come to the table and join in the give and take.

Bargaining is not a good idea in situations where there is a great power disparity between the parties (unless that power disparity is compensated in some way). What may officially be designated as bargaining does not feel like bargaining when one of the parties perceives that it must go along with the proposals suggested by the other. (This is not Negotiating; it is Compelling.)

Finally, bargaining is not a good strategy to use when any of the parties has a high level of fear and perceptual distortion about the other and the situation. This is a condition in which Negotiation is not impossible, but in which it is best postponed until all sides feel a modicum of safety and each is able to approach the problems somewhat rationally and with a clear head.

Probable Outcomes of Negotiation

The outcomes of negotiated conflict management are similar to those for Collaboration, except the commitment to the decisions is not quite as strong. The solutions that people come up with seem to suffice, but they don't fully satisfy. Sometimes with negotiated agreements, the parties have to be reminded of their agreements after they have been made. On other occasions because of the lessened commitment to the decisions, the parties may look for chances to revise the decision because they didn't get everything they wanted out of the original decisions.

Support

Many people have learned Support strategies through training in the helping professions. Often these strategies are called communication skills or active listening. The major assumption of this strategy is that the other is the one with the problem. In Collaboration and Negotiation the major assumption is that the parties share responsibility for "fixing" the difficulty. Not so with support. Here the assumption is that the other owns the problem and it is your task *not* to take responsibility for dealing with it, but to help the other deal with his problem while you encourage the other not to be dependent on you and your resources. This kind of strategy would be appropriate in a situation where two parties are in conflict with each other and one or both are trying to get you—a third person—to take a side. If one of the parties complains about the behavior of the other, then it is not your problem—but you can be helpful to one or the other by trying to help him function in a healthy and ethical manner toward the other.

Perhaps another way to define this strategy is to call it a strengthening, encouraging, empowering, or emboldening strategy. It is your task to help the other feel strong enough and fearless enough to deal with her difficulties without getting you to do the work or the "fixing" for her.

How to Support

When someone is under stress, it is important to give her an immediate opportunity to expend some excess energy. We can relieve some of the stress by encouraging the other to express or describe the feelings being experienced. This means that we encourage her to talk, to be angry, or to cry. It will help if you

- make short, neutral statements or ask questions that acknowledge the other's feelings;
- reflect the feeling content of a person's words or actions.

Usually this will reduce the feelings temporarily, allow the other to look at the situation a little more objectively, and facilitate more effective problem solving.

Support can be enhanced by helping the individual to explore whether other issues are bothering her in addition to the "presenting problem." Sometimes a small incident will trigger an unexpectedly strong reaction; in such a case it becomes important to check the possibility that something else is bothering the person, beyond the immediate and obvious situation. Frustrations may have been building up for some time, perhaps only now being expressed. Without encouragement, a person may still be hesitant to discuss the real sources of the frustration.

To find out the real source of a person's stress, it is important to ask neutral, open-ended questions that stimulate the other to talk. If we ask specific or "loaded" questions, we may never get to the source. In this phase it is also important to communicate an acceptance of what the person is saying. If we judge him or make him feel ashamed of his condition, we will compound the problem.

If possible, with the Support strategy[9] one should attempt to help the other adapt to the situation causing conflict. Adaptation can take place in several ways: by taking action to change the self, the environment, or others or by redefining the situation. This means that we help the other by exploring the situation with her and look for ways that changes might be forthcoming. We can suggest alternative modes of action and help the other come up with new ideas for how to deal with the situation.

Mostly, however, Support strategies help the other to feel strong and confident that he can deal with what is out there. Here you function primarily as a cheering section prodding the other to act and to deal with the situation.

To the extent that you try to admonish, judge, warn, order, or bargain with the other, you are likely to hinder your efforts at Supporting—because these strategies essentially require your motivation rather than the other person's to get the needed change and action.

When to Support

The critical issue in choosing Support strategies has to do with the question "Whose problem is it?" If it is not your problem, that is, if it is not your responsibility to deal with it, or you do not want the responsibility for dealing with it, *and it is the responsibility of the other person to do something about it,* then a Support strategy would be in order. Let's say someone came to you (from a neighborhood distant from yours) complaining of neighbors who are noisy at all hours of the night. That is not your problem to solve. But you want to help your friend deal with the issue in the best way possible. You want to strengthen and encourage your friend to do what needs to be done in that particular conflict setting.

It is also appropriate to use Support strategies when the other person is bringing to your relationship troubles and dissatisfactions outside of your relationship with her. For example, your spouse may come home from work annoyed at the events at the office that day. Perhaps she is angry and upset and challenges others in the family and looks as if she is trying "to pick a fight" at home. This is what we call an "unrealistic" conflict, that is, one that does not have a substantive issue in the setting in which the conflict is being engaged. Some writers call this an intrapersonal conflict—one that has more to do with personality than it does with issues that can be dealt with in the relationship. Another example of unrealistic conflict is the tension that comes from a person who is frightened or insecure about matters that do not relate to the conflict at hand.

Support strategies are appropriate to use when you are in a situation where you don't believe the tension is motivated by the issues at hand.

Support strategies are also recommended when you are in conflict with someone who is not willing to come to the table, so to speak, and work the issues that are important to you both. The use of Support tactics to help the other feel safe with you and develop some trust may help establish an environment in which the other may, finally, join with you in a collaborative effort.

Probable Outcomes of Support

Support usually elicits good feelings. We all like to be listened to and cared about.

The potential problem of Support strategies is that the other may be disappointed that you did not take his side. Of course, there are times when we are looking for no more than a friendly and sympathetic ear. But at other times we would like very much to have an advocate, and we are unhappy that the supportive person is only supportive to the extent of being a good listener.

The best outcome from Support strategies is that the supported people are encouraged to be responsible for themselves. While this may not be what the supported person hoped for, it may well be the best thing for all concerned. Instead of helping people stay dependent, a supportive posture encourages them to take responsibility for themselves.

Conclusion

Once you have completed the questionnaire in this booklet, scored your answers, and reviewed the explanations of the scoring, you should have a vocabulary to help you describe your experience in conflict settings. You should not assume that you have a deep insight into your personality. This instrument is not intended to provide such information. It is a guide to reflection on your own perceptions of your behavior and a guide to reflecting on other options you might want to use in future conflicts when they, inevitably, arise.

NOTES

1. Rensis Likert and Jane Gibson Likert, *New Ways of Managing Conflict* (New York: McGraw-Hill, 1976).

2. William G. Dyer, *Strategies for Managing Change* (Boston: Addison-Wesley, 1984).

3. Alan C. Filley, *Interpersonal Conflict Resolution* (Glenview, IL: Scott Foresman, 1975).

4. Gerard I. Nierenberg, *Fundamentals of Negotiating* (New York: Hawthorne Books, 1973).

5. Chester L. Karrass, *Give and Take: The Complete Guide to Negotiating Strategies and Tactics* (New York: Thomas Y. Crowell, 1974).

6. Roger Fisher and William Ury, *Getting to Yes: Negotiating Agreement Without Giving In* (Boston: Houghton Mifflin, 1981).

7. Ibid., 42.

8. Joyce Frost Hocker and William W. Wilmot, *Interpersonal Conflict* (Dubuque: Wm. C. Brown, 1985), 30. (This book is now out in a newer, 4th ed., 1994.)

9. Jerry Robinson, Roy Clifford, and Joke Dewalle, *Stress in Community Groups* (Champaign: University of Illinois Press, 1975). This material has been modified.

The Conflict Inventory

Instructions for filling out this inventory can be found on pages 2 and 3.

1. A.   Using logic I try to convince the other of my position.
    B.   I use whatever authority I have to convince the other of my position.

2. A.   I let others take responsibility for solving the problem.
    B.   I seek the other's help in working out a solution.

3. A.   I try to find a compromise solution.
    B.   I actively listen to the other.

4. A.   I make an effort to win the other over.
    B.   I will make an effort to go along with what the other wants.

5. A.   I remind the other of the justice of my position.
    B.   I show empathy about the other's plight.

6. A.   I try to surface all of the other person's concerns.
    B.   If I give up something, I expect the other to give up something.

7. A.   I press my argument to get points made.
    B.   I attempt to work on all concerns and issues in the open.

8. A.   I assert my rights.
    B.   I will give up some points in exchange for others.

9. A. I try to soothe the other's feelings to preserve our relationship.
   B. I encourage the other to act for him- or herself.

10. A. I tell the other person my ideas.
    B. I propose a middle ground.

11. A. I remind the other I am an authority on the subject we are
dealing with.
    B. To keep the peace, I might sacrifice my own wishes for
those of the other.

12. A. I invite the other to join with me to deal with the differences
between us.
    B. I assume that giving advice creates dependence on me.

13. A. I try to show the other the soundness of my position.
    B. I usually repeat back or paraphrase what the other has said.

14. A. I use the constitution or policy manual as a backup for my
position.
    B. I encourage the other to stay in the conflict with me until
we agree.

15. A. I try to do what is necessary to avoid tension.
    B. If it makes the other happy, I might let him or her retain
some of his or her views.

16. A. I point to the consequences if the other doesn't listen.
    B. I am firm in pursuing my argument.

17. A. I am concerned with satisfying everybody's wishes.
    B. I try to find a fair way for the other to get what he or she
wants.

18. A. I don't try to persuade another about what should be done. I
help the other find his or her own way.
    B. I try to find a fair combination of gains and losses for both
of us.

19. A.   I try to postpone the issue until a later time.
    B.   I try to show the rationality and benefits of my position.

20. A.   I am nonjudgmental about what the other says or does.
    B.   I call on an expert authority to support my case.

21. A.   I try to find an intermediate position.
    B.   I usually seek the other's help in working out a solution.

22. A.   I tell the other about the problem so we can work it out.
    B.   I propose solutions to our problems.

23. A.   I usually ask for more than I expect to get.
    B.   I offer rewards so the other will go along with my point of view.

24. A.   I try not to give advice, only to help the other make up his or her own mind.
    B.   Differences are not always worth worrying about.

25. A.   I calculate how much I can get, knowing I won't get everything.
    B.   I try to gain the other's trust, to get him or her on my side.

26. A.   I sometimes avoid taking positions that would create unpleasantness.
    B.   I withdraw when I don't get my way.

27. A.   I help the other take care of his or her own problems.
    B.   When someone avoids conflict with me, I invite that person to work it out with me.

28. A.   I try to put as little of myself forward as possible, attempting to make use of the strengths of the other.
    B.   I point out the faults in the other's arguments.

29. A.   When someone threatens me, I assume we have a problem and invite that person to work it out with me.
    B.   When I am right, I don't argue much; I just state my position and stand firm.

30. A. I will give in a little so everybody gets something he or she wants.

     B. I try not to hurt the other's feelings.

31. A. I prepare my case before joining the argument.

     B. I admonish the other to do as I say.

32. A. I am considerate of the other's wishes.

     B. If we are at a loss as to how to work an issue through, we ask for a third party.

33. A. To succeed, one needs to be flexible.

     B. In a conflict, one should focus on fact finding.

34. A. I evaluate the positives and negatives of the other's argument.

     B. If the other's position is important to him or her, I would try to meet those wishes.

35. A. It is more important to be right than to be friendly.

     B. I try to help the other feel courage and power to manage his or her own problems.

36. A. I assume we will all be able to come out winners.

     B. I assume conflict management is the art of attaining the possible.

37. A. When opposed, I can usually come up with a counter argument.

     B. I assume we can work a conflict through.

38. A. I emphasize the gravity of the situation.

     B. In a conflict, everybody should come out with something, though not everything that was expected.

39. A. I prefer to postpone unpleasant situations.

     B. I support the other in trying to find his or her way.

40. A.   I defend my ideas.
     B.   I share only that which is helpful to my case.

41. A.   I let others know whether my requirements are being met.
     B.   I want the other to be content.

42. A.   I attempt to define our mutual problems.
     B.   I sympathize with the other's difficulties, but don't take responsibility for them.

43. A.   I usually plan out my argument.
     B.   I express caring toward the other.

44. A.   If it is important, I will put pressure on the other to get what is needed.
     B.   I join with the other to gather data about our problems.

45. A.   I assume relationships are more important than issues.
     B.   I assume that each of us must give up something for the good of the whole.

From *Discover Your Conflict Management Style*, The Alban Institute: 1997. Copyright 1997. All rights reserved.

Score Form

DO NOT READ UNTIL YOU HAVE COMPLETED THE INVENTORY.

Scoring the Conflict Inventory

Circle the letters below that you circled on each item of the questionnaire.

	Persuade	Compel	Avoid/Accommodate	Collaborate	Negotiate	Support
1	A	B				
2			A	B		
3					A	B
4	A		B			
5		A				B
6				A	B	
7	A			B		
8		A			B	
9			A			B
10	A				B	
11		A	B			
12				A		B
13	A					B
14		A		B		
15			A		B	
16	B	A				
17			B	A		
18					B	A
19	B		A			

	Persuade	Compel	Avoid/ Accommodate	Collaborate	Negotiate	Support
20		B				A
21				B	A	
22	B			A		
23		B			A	
24			B			A
25	B				A	
26		B	A			
27				B		A
28	B					A
29		B		A		
30			B		A	
31	A	B				
32			A	B		
33					A	B
34	A		B			
35		A				B
36				A	B	
37	A			B		
38		A			B	
39			A			B
40	A				B	
41		A	B			
42				A		B
43	A					B
44		A		B		
45			A		B	

Total number of items circled in each column:

_____   _____   _____   _____   _____   _____